Silenced No More

A Personal Healing Journey

A Guided Reflection Journal

Erica Young

PEN TO PAPER
PUBLISHING

This journal is intended as a guided reflection tool for personal growth and healing. It is not intended to replace professional counseling, therapy, or medical advice.

Publisher: Pen to Paper Publishing

First Edition

Printed in the United States of America.

<u>This Is For You</u>

This is for you.

For the woman who carried silence longer than she should have.
For the one who learned to survive before she learned to speak.
For the one who is ready—even if she is still afraid.

These pages are not about perfection.
They are about permission.

Permission to tell the truth.
Permission to move slowly.
Permission to heal in the presence of Christ.

You are not late.
You are not too much.
You are not beyond restoration.

This is for you.

Dedication Page

For the woman who survived in silence
and is learning to live in truth.

For the parts of you that were overlooked, dismissed, or
misunderstood.

And for the grace of Jesus Christ, who heals what we once believed
would remain broken forever.

Table of Contents

Opening Letter

How to Use This Journal

Letter to God

Part I
The Girl Who Learned to Hide

Part II
Growing Up Carrying It

Part III
The Breaking Point

Part IV
The Woman Beneath It All

Part V
When the Voice Returns

Final Reflections

About the Author
Continue the Journey

Opening Letter

Before you begin, take a breath.

This journal is not about doing this perfectly.
It is not about uncovering everything at once.
It is not about reliving what hurt you.

It is about creating space.

Space to notice what has been quiet for a long time.
Space to write honestly.
Space to acknowledge what you have carried and what you are learning
to release.

Some pages may feel light.
Others may feel heavy.

You are allowed to pause.
You are allowed to step away.
You are allowed to return when you are ready.

Healing is not a race.

These pages are here to walk beside you as you begin telling the truth—
first to yourself, and then, perhaps, to the world.

How to Use This Journal

There is no right way to move through these pages.

You may start at the beginning, or you may open to the section that feels most relevant to you today.

Some prompts may stir memories.
Some may feel easier to write through than others.

Take your time.

You are not required to answer every question.
You are not required to fill every page.

This journal is not a test.
It is an invitation.

Write what feels honest.
Skip what feels overwhelming.
Return when you are ready.

Let this be a place where truth can breathe.

Letter to God — What I Hope to Receive

A Prayer from My Heart

Before beginning this journey, take a moment to write honestly to God.

You may write about what you are carrying, what you are hoping for, or what you need as you move through these pages.

There is no right way to write here.
Just be honest.

What do you want God to help you with in this season of healing?

PART I

The Girl Who Learned to Hide

"Silence often begins before we understand why."

Silence is rarely random.

It is often learned slowly—sometimes in moments that felt confusing, sometimes in moments that felt frightening, and sometimes in ways that were never spoken out loud.

Before we explore healing, it can be helpful to gently notice where silence first began.

This is not about blaming yourself.

It is about understanding your story.

Before It Changed

Think about a time in your life before something shifted.

Before the confusion.
Before the silence.
Before you began carrying something that felt too heavy for your age.

What do you remember about who you were then?

Where were you?
What did you love?
What made you feel safe?

What did safety feel like in your body?

The First Silence

Many people can remember a moment when something happened that they didn't tell anyone about.

Maybe it felt confusing.
Maybe you thought no one would believe you.
Maybe you were told directly or indirectly to stay quiet.

What was the first thing you remember not saying?

Why did you choose silence?

What did you tell yourself in order to keep going?

When It Felt Off

Sometimes our instincts notice something before we have words for it.

Looking back now, were there moments when something didn't feel right?

Did you question your instincts?

Were you ever told to ignore what you felt, or made to believe that your discomfort didn't matter?

Write about what you remember.

Blurred Lines

When boundaries are unclear, it can create confusion that lingers for years.

Think about moments when you felt unsure about what was happening or what you were expected to accept.

Were you ever made to feel responsible for something that was not yours to carry?

What emotions surface as you reflect on those experiences now?

Pause here.

Notice your breathing.

Take a slow breath in.

Now release it gently.

What emotions are present right now?

Where do you feel them in your body?

What would help you feel steady before continuing?

Scripture Reflection

"He heals the brokenhearted and binds up their wounds."
— Psalm 147:3

What does it mean to consider that healing is possible?

How does this verse speak to where you are today?

What I Have Never Said Out Loud

This is your safe space to say it now.

PART II

Growing Up Carrying It

"Survival carried you then—now you are learning what you no longer have to carry."

What once helped you survive may now feel heavy.

The habits, patterns, and ways of protecting yourself that formed in earlier seasons often remain long after the moment has passed.

This does not mean you did anything wrong.

It means you adapted.

In this section, you are simply noticing what you carried forward—and how those experiences may have shaped the woman you became.

You are not criticizing who you were.

You are honoring how you survived.

The Mask I Wore

Many people learn to appear strong long before they feel strong.

Sometimes the world only sees the version of us that functions well, works hard, smiles often, and keeps moving forward.

But underneath that strength, there may have been emotions you never felt safe expressing.

What role did you learn to play in order to survive?

Were you the strong one?
The responsible one?
The quiet one?
The one who never caused trouble?

What did people believe about you that wasn't the full truth?

My Body Remembers

Even when memories fade, the body often remembers.

Experiences that once felt overwhelming can show up later as tension, anxiety, or emotional reactions we struggle to explain.

This is not weakness.

It is the body responding to what it once endured.

Where do you notice tension in your body when you feel stressed or triggered?

Are there certain situations, conversations, or environments that make you feel uneasy?

What does anxiety feel like in your body?

What helps your body feel calm or grounded again?

Anger I Wasn't Allowed to Feel

Anger is often misunderstood.

Many people who experienced difficult or confusing situations growing up were never given permission to feel angry.

Instead, they were told to stay quiet, be respectful, forgive quickly, or move on.

But anger can also be a signal.

It can point to places where something important was ignored, crossed, or dismissed.

In this space, you are allowed to write honestly.

What situations from your past still stir anger when you think about them?

Were there moments when you wanted to speak up but didn't feel safe doing so?

What would you say now if you could speak freely?

There is no need to censor yourself here.

Pause for a moment.

Take a slow breath.

You have already done something courageous by reflecting on experiences that may have been buried for a long time.

What emotions are present right now?

What feels different after writing?

What would bring comfort or steadiness in this moment?

Body Awareness

Place your hand over your heart.

Notice your breathing.

There is no need to rush forward.

What does your body need right now?

Rest?
Stillness?
Movement?
Quiet?

Write whatever feels true in this moment.

What I Am Beginning to Understand About Myself

Write it down so you can hold on to it.

PART III

The Breaking Point

"What was buried begins to rise when silence can no longer hold it."

There are moments when the story we have been carrying quietly begins to surface.

Sometimes it happens through a conversation.
Sometimes through a memory.
Sometimes through exhaustion from holding everything in for too long.

What once felt distant or buried suddenly feels closer.

This moment is not about reliving what hurt you.

It is about allowing truth to have a voice.

The Moment I Knew

For many people, there comes a moment when something shifts.

A moment when what was once confusing begins to make sense. A moment when silence no longer feels sustainable.

Can you remember a time when you began to see your story differently?

What happened that made you realize something needed to be acknowledged or understood more clearly?

What emotions surfaced when that awareness came?

Naming It

Sometimes the hardest part of healing is simply finding the words.

For years, many people avoid certain language because it feels too heavy, too final, or too painful to say.

But naming an experience does not give it power over you.

It simply allows truth to exist.

Are there words you have avoided when thinking about your story?

What feels difficult to name even now?

What would it feel like to acknowledge those words honestly?

What I Believed About Myself

Experiences shape more than memories.

They often shape the beliefs we quietly carry about who we are.

Sometimes we begin to believe things that were never meant to define us.

Take a moment to reflect.

Did you ever feel responsible?
Unworthy?
Invisible?
Ashamed?

What Happened

Write about the experience or memory that feels most important to acknowledge today.

What I Believed About Myself

What story did you begin telling yourself because of it?

Truth Reflection

Now consider a different question.

If what happened to you does not define who you are, what might be true instead?

What would it look like to separate your identity from the experiences you endured?

Write about the truths you are beginning to discover.

Scripture Reflection

"Then you will know the truth, and the truth will set you free."
— John 8:32

What does it mean to you that truth has the power to bring freedom?

How might honesty about your story open the door to healing?

What I Am Ready to Release

Draw, journal, or color it out right here.

PART IV

The Woman Beneath It All

"Beneath everything you carried, you were still there."

Beneath the silence.
Beneath the coping.
Beneath the survival patterns you learned along the way...

You are still there.

Not erased.
Not ruined.
Not defined only by what you endured.

This part of the journey is about rediscovering who you are beneath everything you carried.

Healing does not erase your story.

It reminds you that your story is not the only thing that defines you.

Before the Silence

Before the moments that changed you, there was a younger version of you who experienced the world differently.

She had interests, dreams, and parts of her personality that existed before survival became necessary.

What do you remember about who you were before things shifted?

What did you enjoy?
What made you feel curious or excited?
What parts of your personality felt natural and free?

Write about the girl you once were.

Despite Everything

Even in difficult circumstances, some parts of us refuse to disappear.

Strength can exist quietly beneath the surface for years before we recognize it.

Looking back now, what qualities helped you continue moving forward?

What strengths allowed you to keep going even when things felt overwhelming?

Consider moments when you showed courage, resilience, or determination—even if you didn't realize it at the time.

Identity Beyond Survival

For a long time, survival may have shaped how you saw yourself.

But survival is not the whole story.

Who are you beyond what happened to you?

What qualities do you see in yourself today that reflect growth, strength, or wisdom?

How has your story shaped you in ways that reveal perseverance or compassion?

Identity Reflection

Complete these statements in your own words.

I am not _______________________________.

I am _______________________________.

I am becoming _______________________________.

Faith Reflection

Sometimes healing invites us to reconsider what we believe about ourselves in light of what God says is true.

What does it mean to consider that your worth was never determined by what happened to you?

What truths about your identity are you beginning to understand more clearly?

Scripture Reflection

"I praise you because I am fearfully and wonderfully made."
— Psalm 139:14

What does it mean to reflect on this verse as part of your healing journey?

How might this truth shape the way you see yourself moving forward?

I Am Still Here

What does this mean to you?

PART V

When the Voice Returns

"The same voice that learned to be quiet is now learning to speak."

There is a difference between surviving and living.

For a long time, survival may have required silence, distance, or emotional protection.

But healing often begins when your voice starts to return.

Your voice does not have to be loud to be real.

Sometimes it sounds like honesty.
Sometimes it sounds like boundaries.
Sometimes it sounds like peace.

In this section, you are invited to reflect on what it means to move forward with strength and clarity.

If I Wasn't Afraid

Fear can keep us quiet long after danger has passed.

But when fear loosens its grip, truth often begins to rise.

Take a moment to imagine what your life might look like if fear had less control over your voice.

If I wasn't afraid, I would say...

If I wasn't afraid, I would stop pretending...

If I wasn't afraid, I would ask for...

Write freely and honestly.

Boundaries I Am Learning

Healing often includes recognizing what you will and will not allow in your life moving forward.

Boundaries are not punishment.

They are protection.

They create space for safety, honesty, and respect.

Reflect on what you are learning about boundaries in your life.

I no longer need to tolerate ___________________.

I am learning to say no when ___________________.

Healthy boundaries in my life might look like ___________________.

The Woman I Am Becoming

Healing does not mean forgetting the past.

It means recognizing that your story is still unfolding.

Who do you see yourself becoming as you continue moving forward?

What qualities do you want to grow stronger in your life?

What hopes or dreams feel possible now that once felt distant?

Write about the woman you are becoming.

A Letter to My Younger Self

Imagine speaking to the younger version of yourself who first experienced the moments that shaped your story.

What would you want her to know today?

What comfort, truth, or reassurance would you offer her now?

A Letter to the Woman I Am Becoming

Now imagine writing to the version of yourself who continues walking forward in healing.

What encouragement would you offer her?

What promises do you want to keep as you continue growing?

Reflection

Take a moment to pause.

Look back at what you have written in these pages.

What have you learned about yourself?

What truths feel clearer now?

What strength have you noticed in your own story?

Letter to God — What I Want to Say Now

A Prayer of Gratitude and Hope

Return to God with the thoughts and feelings you carry at the end of this reflection journey.

What has changed for you?

What are you grateful for?

What are you still asking for as you continue walking forward?

Write honestly from your heart.

My Next Steady Step

There is no need to rush forward.

Healing is not a single moment.
It is a series of small, steady choices.

What feels like the next wise step for you?

You showed up.

You allowed yourself to reflect, to remember, and to write honestly.

That takes courage.

Healing is not about erasing the past.

It is about learning that what happened to you does not get the final word.

Your story continues.

And the woman who walks forward from here carries both truth and strength.

You are not defined by silence.

You are becoming.

You were never meant to carry silence alone.

You are not behind.
You are not too late.
You are not too broken.

You are becoming.

"He heals the brokenhearted
and binds up their wounds."
— Psalm 147:3

About the Author

Erica Young is a writer, educator, and trauma-informed coach who is passionate about helping individuals find their voice, tell their stories, and walk in healing.

Having overcome her share of trauma from childhood into adulthood, Erica understands firsthand what it means to carry silence, to navigate the weight of unspoken experiences, and to begin the journey toward truth and restoration. Her work is rooted in both personal experience and a deep commitment to creating safe spaces where others can reflect, write, and grow without pressure or judgment.

As a professional editor, author coach, and college instructor, Erica has helped many individuals move from uncertainty to clarity—guiding them as they share their stories with honesty, purpose, and dignity. She believes that healing and writing are deeply connected, and that giving language to our experiences can be a powerful step toward freedom.

This journal was created as a companion to *The Lost Woman: Silenced No More*, offering a guided space for reflection, processing, and personal growth. Erica's heart is that these pages help you feel seen, supported, and encouraged as you continue your journey.

Continue the Journey

Healing is not a single moment—it is a journey that unfolds one step at a time.

If this journal has helped you reflect on your story, you may find additional support and encouragement through the following resources.

The Memoir

The Lost Woman: Silenced No More
A deeply personal story of surviving childhood trauma and discovering healing through truth, faith, and courage.

Writing With Dignity and Grace

A program designed to help individuals tell their stories with honesty and purpose.

Overcoming 2 Become

A nonprofit committed to supporting survivors on their healing journey through resources, encouragement, and community.

For additional resources, visit:
www.ericatrinette.com

www.overcoming2become.org